Words of Advice

A GUIDEBOOK
FOR FAMILIES
SERVING AS
ADVISORS

JOSIE THOMAS

ELIZABETH S. JEPPSON

INSTITUTE FOR FAMILY-CENTERED CARE
With support from the Maternal & Child Health Bureau
U.S. Department of Health & Human Services

The Institute for Family-Centered Care is a non-profit organization providing essential leadership to advance the understanding and practice of family-centered care. By promoting collaborative, empowering relationships between providers and consumers, the Institute facilitates family-centered change in all settings where individuals and families receive care and support.

The Institute serves as a central resource for policy makers, administrators, program planners, direct service providers, educators, design professionals, and family members. Institute staff promote change and enhance the quality of health and other human services through development of print and audiovisual resources, information dissemination, policy and research initiatives, training, and technical assistance.

To cite this publication:

Thomas, J. & Jeppson, E. S. (1997), *Words of advice: A guidebook for families serving as advisors*. Bethesda, MD: Institute for Family-Centered Care.

ISBN 0-9642014-1-0

Copyright ©1997 Institute for Family-Centered Care

Cover Illustration by Katherine Van Horne
Publication Design & Layout by Catherine Scruggs

Table of Contents

Introduction 1
Why Should You Become an Advisor? 3
The Advisory Roles Consumers Play 4
Benefits to Being an Advisor 6
Challenges to Being an Advisor 11
Making It Happen 16
    Identify Your Strengths
    Gather Information
    Sell Yourself
    Get Support
    Build Your Skills
    Plan for Challenges
Serving as an Advisor: Six Roles You Can Play 42
    If You're Serving on an Advisory Board or Committee
    If You're Attending a Conference
    If You're Providing Training
    If You're Testifying to Legislators
    If You're Supporting Other Families
    If You're Considering a Paid Staff or Consultant Position
Ready or Not? 15 Questions to Ask Yourself 73
In Conclusion 75
Who are the Advisors? 77
Resources 79

Many colleagues shared their ideas and experiences in the development and review of this publication. We especially want to acknowledge and thank the following family members and professionals who generously gave their time to review drafts of this publication.

Betsy Boggs	Phyllis Landry	Bill Stumpf
Katie Bond	Terri Mitchell	Janice Tanner
Sarah Colston	Sarah O'Brien	Glenn Turner
Evelyn Hausslein	Bruce Orr	Conni Wells
Felicia Jordan		

Introduction

"Hello. Is this Maria Evans? We're looking for a family member to serve on an advisory committee at our hospital. You were recommended by several people. Can you do it?"

As a parent of a child with special needs, or as a consumer of services yourself, you may have received a phone call just like this one. You may have been invited to review and comment on educational materials being developed for children and their families. Or you may have been nominated to serve on a statewide interagency council developing services for infants and toddlers with developmental delays. You may even have decided to apply for a paid position as a peer consultant at the hospital where you received treatment for cancer.

As programs and organizations embrace the concepts of family-centered care, more and more family members* are sharing their experiences and expertise with program planners and policy makers. While these new advisory roles are a welcome opportunity for both consumers and providers, they also involve adjusting to new ways of working together and, often, learning new skills. Neither family members nor providers may fully understand the role of the consumer advisor or what is required to make it a success.

If you have never served in an advisory role, but think you might find it interesting and rewarding, this workbook is for you. It offers guidance for thinking through the benefits and demands of advisory roles for consumers, presents some fundamental principles for being a successful advisor, and suggests practical tips for dealing with the common challenges that families encounter in these new roles. It also includes ideas and self-assessment activities to help you identify the skills you bring to the advisory relationship, and to recognize the supports you may need to participate successfully. Finally, it includes the thoughts, observations, and suggestions of family members from around the country who are already participating as advisors. Their "words of advice" are a rich source of wisdom and support.

We hope you will find the steps outlined in this book helpful as you consider taking on an advisory role. Remember, however, that becoming an effective advisor is a process. Family members don't learn of their child's special needs one day, wake up the next and say, "Okay, I think I'll join the hospital's Parent Advisory Council." Typically their energies first go into learning about their child's needs, collaborating with professionals to develop a plan of care that is consistent with their family's values and priorities, and building a support network with other families in their community. Only after these essential information and support needs are met should family members consider taking on an advisory role.

Of course, not every parent of a child with special needs decides to serve as a policy or program advisor. Just as every child is unique, so too is every family and every family member. Different activities or levels of involvement and different roles appeal to different people. That diversity of interests is what makes life so interesting! If you do decide to share your expertise as an advisor, however, we hope you will find it a rewarding and fun experience.

Throughout this book the terms family members, parents, and consumers are used interchangeably. In all cases they refer to those whose initial interaction with the service system is as a consumer of services. The information presented in this publication is applicable both for parents whose children receive services and for adults who are consumers of services.

Why Should You Become An Advisor?

As the parent of a child with special needs, or as a consumer of adult services, you are uniquely qualified to offer providers, administrators, program planners, and policy makers information about what works and what doesn't work for you and your family. You can offer fresh insights on what it's really like to receive services from a particular program or agency. You know how it feels to wait in an overcrowded waiting room, or to hear bad news over the telephone. You also know how it feels to have a caring nurse or therapist spend extra time helping you understand something particularly difficult about your child's care.

You are the expert on the experience of being a service consumer. You bring the perspective that providers and policy makers do not have—the perspective of someone very close to the system but not constrained by the traditions of the system. Providers, policy makers, and program planners need the type of information you have to develop programs and services that really meet families' needs and priorities.

Words of Advice...
from Geneva Morrison

Professionals began asking me to speak to doctors and other providers about my experiences. I started to tell my story to small groups of professionals at workshops and training sessions. I realized I could help shape their understanding of the importance of collaborating with families.

The Advisory Roles Consumers Play

Today, many programs, organizations, and agencies are actively seeking ways to increase family involvement in policy and program development and evaluation. Your child's school, hospital, or early intervention program, the county or state health agency, national organizations, and even the federal government are all developing opportunities for consumers to have a greater voice in shaping service systems.

There are many, many kinds of advisory roles that consumers can play. Most people think of a formal task force or committee when talking about "consumers as advisors." But we think the concept is really much broader. We use the term "advisor" to describe *any* role that enables families to have direct input and influence on the way care and services are organized and delivered.

Table 1—Advisory Roles Consumers Can Play presents some of the advisory roles and functions consumers can perform.

Table 1

ADVISORY ROLES CONSUMERS CAN PLAY

- Members of task forces
- Advisory board members
- Program evaluators
- Co-trainers for preservice or inservice sessions
- Paid program staff
- Paid program or policy consultants
- Mentors for other families
- Grant reviewers
- Reviewers of audiovisual and written materials
- Providing testimony at hearings
- Advocates
- Participants in focus groups
- Members of committees hiring new staff
- Fund raisers
- Members of boards of trustees/boards of directors
- Participants at conferences and working meetings
- Participants in quality improvement initiatives

Source: Jeppson, E. S. & Thomas, J. (1995). *Essential Allies: Families as Advisors.* Bethesda, MD: Institute for Family-Centered Care.

Benefits to Being an Advisor

You may be thinking, "Great! But why should I do it?" Parents who choose to get involved beyond the individual care level, say there are enormous benefits for themselves, for providers, and for programs serving children and families as a result of their involvement. Families say that when they serve in advisory roles they can help change people's attitudes about children with special needs and their families. They say it broadens their own outlook and helps them see beyond the needs of their own child and family. And, they say they can help to create services and programs that are truly responsive to children and families. Listed in *Table 2—When Families Serve As Advisors* are some other benefits identified by families.

> *Words of Advice...*
> **from Nancy DiVenere**
>
> *Knowing I had the opportunity to influence one discussion or make one point that couldn't or wouldn't have been made without my presence as a family member is success.*

Table 2

WHEN FAMILIES SERVE AS ADVISORS

Benefits For Families

- ✔ It improves services for my child and for other children.
- ✔ It provides an opportunity to bring about meaningful change.
- ✔ It increases opportunities for me to share information with other parents.
- ✔ It feels good to make a contribution.
- ✔ It is satisfying to give back to the system.
- ✔ It provides opportunities to network with other consumers and providers.
- ✔ It expands my knowledge and skills.

Benefits For Providers:

- ✔ It improves the planning process.
- ✔ It helps them carry out the mission of the program.
- ✔ It increases their knowledge and skills.
- ✔ It helps them do their job better.
- ✔ It brings fresh perspectives to problems.
- ✔ It provides an ally to advocate for better services for children and families.
- ✔ It increases their empathy for and understanding of families.

On the next page is *Activity 1—Families As Advisors: What's In It For Me.* This activity will help you think about the benefits that accrue when families work as partners with providers at the program and policy level.

In the left-hand column, list the benefits to you and your family, in the middle column list the benefits to the families you know, and in the right-hand column list the benefits to providers and to programs when families are involved in advisory roles.

Activity 1
FAMILIES AS ADVISORS: WHAT'S IN IT FOR ME

Benefits to Me and My Family	Benefits to Other Families	Benefits to Providers/Programs

Adapted from Edelman, L. E. (1991). *Getting on board: Training activities to promote the practice of family-centered care.* Bethesda, MD: Association for the Care of Children's Health.

Now that you have identified the benefits to you and to the providers you know, use *Activity 2—Ask Yourself These Questions*, to think about your own involvement as an advisor.

Activity 2
ASK YOURSELF THESE QUESTIONS

- Will my involvement make a difference for my child and my family?   ❑ Yes   ❑ No

- Will my participation make a difference to the families I know?   ❑ Yes   ❑ No

- Will my participation have an impact on the way services are being planned and delivered for children and their families?   ❑ Yes   ❑ No

- Is this worth my time?   ❑ Yes   ❑ No

Remember to reflect on these questions each time you are asked to serve in an advisory role.

My thoughts:

_____

_____

_____

_____

Challenges to Being an Advisor

Opportunities to work together in new ways with providers can also create challenges. These challenges may be related to programmatic or institutional structures, to family and professional attitudes, or to personal responsibilities or family illness.

Many organizations have regulations and procedures that are bureaucratic and inflexible, making it difficult for parents to get the support they need to participate effectively. Agencies may not have developed an adequate system to provide reimbursement or other supports for families. An organization's lack of support for child care or respite care, or its inability to provide transportation or reimbursement for out-of-pocket costs, may make it difficult for you to participate as much as you would like.

At times your own or your child's illness or your job responsibilities may not permit you to participate as freely or fully as you would like. In addition, if professionals are skeptical about parent participation in policy development and program planning, it may be hard to become involved in a meaningful way.

Words of Advice...
from Virginia Ross

I set personal goals for myself, and try not to be pressured to do more than I'm ready for. I'm giving 100% moving at my own pace.

INSTITUTE FOR FAMILY-CENTERED CARE

Can you identify what might make it difficult for you to participate? What are your time and energy limitations? Will you need child care, respite care, or financial support? What are some of the attitudes that you might encounter that will not be helpful—your own as well as others? What are some of the policies and rules that might get in the way?

List these in *Activity 3—My Challenges To Being An Advisor.* Then list some of the strategies you can use to overcome these barriers. You can think about these questions each time you undertake a new advisory role.

Activity 3
MY CHALLENGES TO BEING AN ADVISOR

What might get in the way of my participation as an advisor?

What steps can I take to address these barriers?

Words of Advice...
from Katie Bond

It was difficult suddenly being asked to advocate not just for my child but for a broader contingent. I struggle with those two roles all the time, but it's part of the territory and needs to be acknowledged.

Here is a list of barriers that other family members have identified:

- Lack of support such as reimbursement for expenses, child care, or transportation
- Inconvenient meeting times or locations
- Being the only consumer in an advisory role for an agency
- Not knowing how much to reveal about myself, my child, and my family
- Feeling intimidated
- Not understanding the system's or organization's structure
- No peers within the system to confide in or talk with
- Conflicts with professionals who feel threatened by these new roles
- Changes in peer relationships, or jealousy from other parent friends
- Expectations from others to do more
- Feelings of fatigue or hopelessness when changes don't happen
- Difficulties balancing family and advisory roles

Recognizing the advantages and costs to your participation can help you make decisions about taking on an advisory role. Talk over the benefits as well as the barriers with your family, friends, and providers. Think about whether the challenges are manageable and identify the supports you may need to be successful. If you decide to take on an advisory role, be sure to re-examine your commitment from time to time. Do the advantages of being an advisor still outweigh the demands?

My thoughts:

_____

_____

_____

_____

_____

_____

_____

_____

_____

_____

Making It Happen

Whether you want to become involved as a volunteer on an advisory committee that is planning a new hospital, a state interagency coordinating council (ICC), or in a paid position in a health department, making it happen requires commitment from you, your family, and professionals. Your decision to become involved at the policy level should be made with your entire family because, often, these types of roles can involve time away from home, placing caregiving responsibilities on other members of your family. It also requires some thoughtful planning and dialogue with providers to be sure that everything you will need to be successful is discussed and planned for ahead of time. Key steps to preparing yourself for an advisory role are presented below.

> ## Words of Advice...
> *from Conni Wells*
>
> *When someone asks you to become involved as an advisor, you don't have to respond immediately. Take some time before making a decision. Tell them you'd like to think it over for a few days and you'll get back to them.*

Before Your Serve in an Advisory Role

1. Identify your strengths
2. Gather information
3. Sell yourself
4. Get support
5. Build your skills
6. Plan for challenges

Identify Your Strengths

When asked to serve in an advisory role, some parents ask, "Why are you asking me? I'm just a parent." But, are you really just a parent? Without realizing it, you may demonstrate every day the qualities of leadership and the necessary skills to be a successful advisor. And remember, the most important thing you bring to an advisory role is your experience as a consumer of services. Your perspective is unique!

In a recent survey, families in advisory roles identified the qualities and skills that helped them be successful. These qualities are listed on the next page in *Activity 4—Characteristics of a Successful Advisor*. Circle the ones that describe you.

You'll notice that skills such as typing, writing, using a computer, and even public speaking do not appear on the list of qualities that families said were essential to their roles as advisors. Of course, those skills can be useful—but they can also be easily learned if, and when, they are needed. More important are qualities such as commitment, optimism, and most of all an attitude of partnership and collaboration. Use *Activity 5—A Checklist for Effective Collaboration* to think about the attitudes and strengths you bring to the role of advisor.

Activity 4
CHARACTERISTICS OF A SUCCESSFUL ADVISOR

- Able to communicate well
- Able to listen well
- Able to network
- Understand my own child's needs
- Work well with others
- Commitment
- Organized
- Optimism
- Confidence
- Caring
- Experience working with other parents
- Able to provide and receive support
- Non judgmental
- Sense of humor
- Willing to share life experiences
- Desire to help others
- Acceptance of self and others
- Outgoing
- Ability to speak comfortably about own situation
- Willing to learn
- Can ask for help
- Able to share
- Able to interact with many different kinds of people
- Understand children and families beyond my own child
- Honest
- Attitude of partnership

WORDS OF ADVICE

Activity 5
A CHECKLIST FOR EFFECTIVE COLLABORATION

	YES	NO
Ability to see strengths in myself		
Do I believe that I bring a unique perspective to the relationship with providers?	❏	❏
Do I believe that families' perspectives and opinions are as important as providers?	❏	❏
Ability to provide support to others		
Am I willing to share my own experience?	❏	❏
Am I nonjudgmental?	❏	❏
Am I coping well with my own emotional issues?	❏	❏
Can I identify the needs and feelings of others?	❏	❏
Ability to work with other families		
Am I willing to become involved with other families?	❏	❏
Can I handle confidential information without discussing it with others?	❏	❏
Am I a good listener?	❏	❏
Can I work with little praise and recognition?	❏	❏
Can I give to others without expecting something in return?	❏	❏
Ability to work collaboratively		
Do I treat each provider as an individual and avoid letting past negative experiences or negative attitudes get in the way of establishing good working relationships?	❏	❏
Am I able to work in partnership, even when I disagree?	❏	❏
When I have a positive relationship with a professional or an agency, do I express support for that person or agency?	❏	❏
Do I maintain realistic expectations for myself and for the providers I work with?	❏	❏
Am I able to wear two hats—that of a consumer and that of an agency representative?	❏	❏

Adapted from Family Support Network of Michigan (1994). *Support parent training: Facilitator's guide.* Michigan Department of Public Health, Children's Special Health Services, Parent Participation Program.

Now that you have learned more about your own strengths and attitudes, it's important to think about the issues and types of advisory roles that appeal to you. *Activity 6—What Do I Bring To The Advisory Role* presents some questions to help narrow your focus, identify your interests, and determine your level of commitment.

Activity 6
WHAT DO I BRING TO THE ADVISORY ROLE?

1. What issues interest me the most?

2. What boards, committees, or other parent consultant positions are most likely to deal with these issues?

3. Who can help me find out about getting involved?

WHAT DO I BRING TO THE ADVISORY ROLE? (cont.)

4. What do I hope to achieve from participating as an advisor?

5. What skills and knowledge do I hope to gain from this experience?

6. How much time and energy do I have to give to this position?

7. What do I need to learn to be effective?

8. Who can help support me in this role?

Adapted from Hunter, R. W. (1994). *Parents as policy-makers: A handbook for effective participation.* Portland State University, Research and Training Center on Family Support and Children's Mental Health.

Gather Information

Before becoming involved as an advisor with an organization, learn as much as you can about it—the organization's mission and vision, the people involved, and most importantly, what's expected of you.

Words of Advice...
from Bev Crider

The most important thing is to do your homework....Learn about what exists.

For example:

- Learn about the history of the organization. Ask for things in writing and read them. Ask for organizational charts, bylaws, mission and vision statements, minutes from past meetings, reports, and parent handbooks.

- Visit the program or agency during the day to observe the program in action.

- Talk to staff and find out how they relate to families.

- Talk to families who receive services from the agency to learn their perspectives about the organization.

- Talk to other family members already serving as advisors to the organization.

- Find out who the decision makers are. Would consumer advisors have contact with them?

- Talk to community leaders to learn their perceptions of the organization.

- Attend a committee meeting.

My thoughts:

_____
_____
_____
_____
_____
_____
_____
_____

Words of Advice...
from the staff of Pilot Parent Partnerships

Be sure to get a feel for the agency's overall philosophy about consumers as advisors. Also, think about the organization's vision—does it fit with your personal vision? Protect your personal boundaries—it's okay to say no.

Sell Yourself

If you've decided you would like to serve as an advisor there are some simple steps that will help you establish such a role.

Network with other parents and providers to learn what is available. Talk with other parents and consumers about your ideas. Ask them what they would find helpful about having a consumer serve in an advisory role. Talk to providers about families as advisors. Ask them if they are currently involved in any collaborative activities with families. Contact heads of agencies and organizations to see if they have developed advisory positions or opportunities. Find out about policies that recommend or promote consumer involvement.

Participate in agency activities to make yourself known. If your children's hospital holds resource fairs, support group meetings, consumer breakfasts, or NICU reunions, be sure to attend and meet people there. Let them know you are interested in becoming involved. If there is a volunteer program, give some of your time to become more knowledgeable about the program and to get to know the staff.

Say that you are interested in working in an advisory role. Let people know that you would like to get involved in an advisory role. If you are looking for a paid position, ask who you should talk to about interviewing for such a position.

Develop a resumé using your family experiences (see page 71). Whether you are looking for a paid position or a volunteer advisory role, it's a good idea to prepare a resume that highlights your experiences as a consumer of services.

Get Support

Any consumer advisor, whether it's a veteran parent who has worked for years in a paid parent consultant position or a family member who has been newly appointed to a consumer advisory committee, needs support. The support and help of your family, friends, other consumers, and providers are key to your success as an advisor.

Identifying Your Personal Supports

Write the names of people you know in the circles in *Activity 7—My Support Team*. Underline the names of those you think you can rely on to help you in your advisory role. These people are resources to you. Building strong relationships with the people you have underlined will help you achieve your goal of being a successful advisor.

Words of Advice...
from Molly Cole

Sometimes, the family advocate role is very lonely. Our triumphs may not be viewed as successes by the people or policies that we challenge...talking with others helps a lot.

Activity 7
MY SUPPORT TEAM

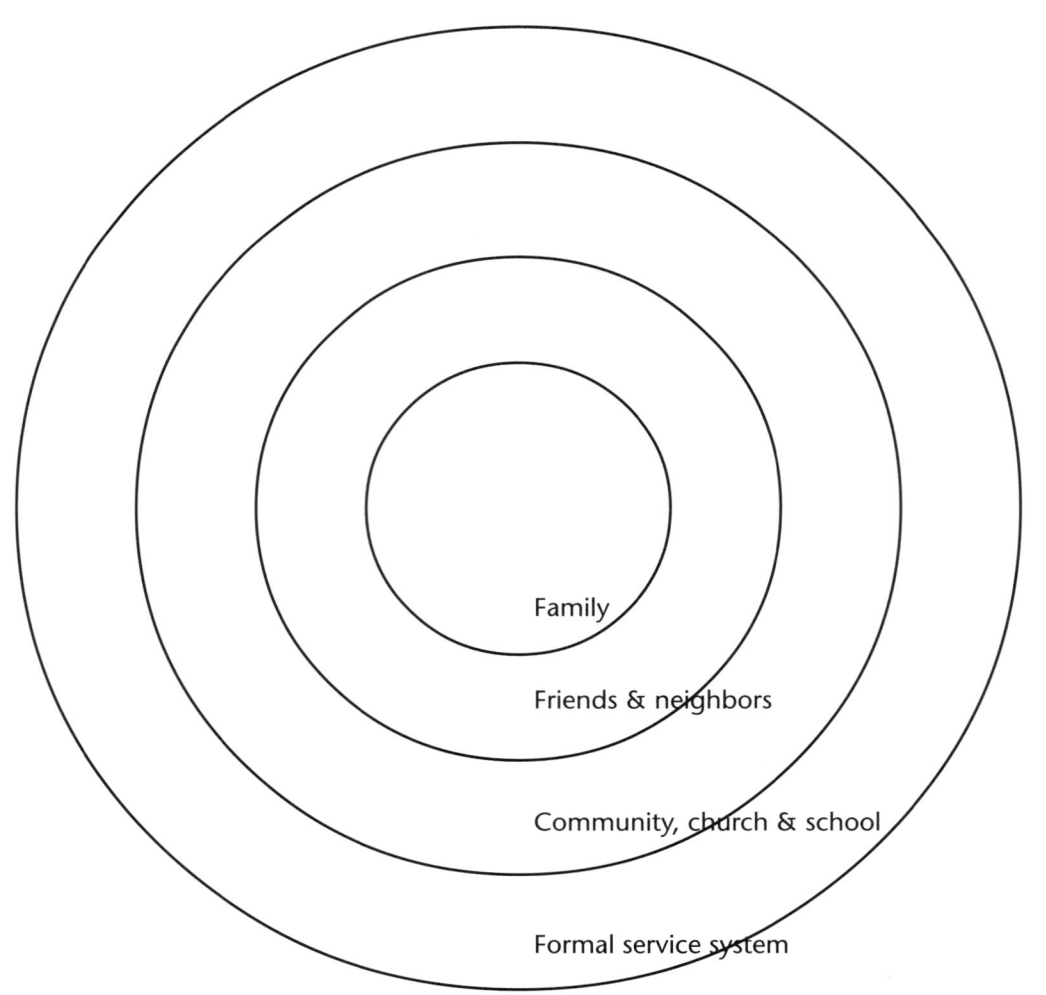

Networking

Family members who serve as advisors say that staying connected to other consumers helps them stay focused on what's really important. Meeting with other families of children with special needs and talking with other consumers gives you a constituency for sharing ideas and getting feedback. As a consumer advisor you are representing the ideas, concerns, and experiences of many families. It is essential that you stay in touch with them.

Networking with other families, especially those in similar roles, can also help reduce the sense of loneliness that sometimes comes with being an advisor. As with any new position, you have to prove yourself as capable and knowledgeable. This may be particularly difficult if there is skepticism about the value of having consumers serve as advisors, or if the organization has never before had a family member on a committee or staff. At those times, a network of colleagues and friends is an invaluable resource.

Words of Advice...
from Faye Eldar

If you find yourself with little supervision or support in your new role, enlist a few friends in the field and talk to them regularly. Use them as a sounding board to discuss issues and dilemmas and to problem-solve.

In *Activity 8—Families Who Make A Difference,* list the people you regard as successful advocates for their children and themselves. Add all the consumers you know who serve in advisory roles. Include these names in your list of people who are resources to you. They can help you understand issues, offer feedback, and provide information to increase your effectiveness as an advisor. Talking with them on occasion to share ideas and resolve difficulties can be an important source of support.

Activity 8
FAMILIES WHO MAKE A DIFFERENCE

1.

2.

3.

4.

In addition to the support of family, friends, and colleagues you may require other practical and emotional supports in your new role. *Table 3— Planning For Success: The Supports Families Need* lists some of the supports consumers have said they need in order to be effective advisors.

Words of Advice...
from Molly Cole

Stay focused and do what you can do well.

Table 3

PLANNING FOR SUCCESS: THE SUPPORTS FAMILIES NEED

❑ Adequate and timely reimbursement—for child care, travel expenses, and time

❑ A designated staff person to help with reimbursement and other issues

❑ Mentoring from an experienced family advocate

❑ Access to timely, clear, and appropriate information

❑ A clear description of roles and responsibilities

❑ Opportunities to develop meaningful relationships with other families and with professionals

❑ Opportunities to network with peers locally, in other states, or nationally

❑ Option to take "time off" if needed while still maintaining membership on the committee or task force.

Build Your Skills

As an advisor, you may be asked to participate in activities you've never been involved in before. These might include attending committee meetings, participating in conferences, or even providing training to other families and to professionals. These activities may be "old hat" to some consumers and brand new for others. Opportunities to build your skills in new areas may be offered as part of your advisory role, or may require taking a class or participating in a training session to broaden your knowledge and understanding.

Although, it is often not necessary to develop office or public speaking skills to be an effective advisor, some family members feel that they would benefit from learning how to use a computer, write a grant, run a meeting, or communicate more effectively. Many such courses can be relatively inexpensive and are available in local community colleges, in high school adult education classes, and in local parent organizations. Take advantage of them.

Words of Advice...
from Geneva Morrison

The more involved I became in advisory activities, the more I realized I needed to learn to be successful. I enrolled in a program for community activists where I learned computer skills and improved my public speaking. Most communities offer these kinds of free or low-cost courses. A six week course on grant writing at my local community college costs only $15.

Words of Advice...
from Conni Wells

If you don't feel ready to take on a large advisory role, develop your skills by participating in a preliminary role. For example, attend a conference as a participant rather than as a speaker.

Telling Your Story

A skill you will use often in your role as an advisor is story-telling. Family leaders are frequently asked to share their stories. These stories are an important and precious resource for family members in their advisory, leadership, and support activities.

Your story of your experiences with the service system can be a powerful tool for bringing about constructive change. When you share your story with providers and policy makers you deepen their understanding of the issues, increase their sensitivity to children and families, and help them make decisions that lead to more supportive policies and practices.

As an advisor you will have the opportunity to share your family's story in many different circumstances and settings. You may be asked to tell your story at a committee or advisory board meeting. You may be invited to speak to a group of providers-in-training, to give a formal presentation at a conference, or to provide testimony to elected officials.

The way you present your story can have a long term effect on the way people view you, your child and family, and other families in similar circumstances. Therefore, it is important to give some serious thought to why and how you want to tell your story.

> *Words of Advice...*
> *from Geneva Morrison*
>
> *I started telling my story. The more I shared it, the more healing I received for myself.*

Before you agree to tell your story, consider the following questions:

- What am I willing to share?
- What do I feel is too private to share?
- What does my family not want me to talk about?
- What will my story teach those who are listening?

It is very important to think through these questions and issues before you are called on to share your personal experiences. Sometimes reliving these private family experiences can be painful. Planning ahead for what you will share, and how you will share it, will help you feel more comfortable when the time comes to tell about an event in your family's life. Remember, your story is a precious resource—use it thoughtfully and wisely.

Words of Advice...
from Mona Freedman

We begin every Interagency Coordinating Council meeting with a family story. I think it helps build trust between families and providers, and reminds us of the real purpose of our work.

Before you agree to tell your story, you should also gather as much information as possible about what is expected of you and what you can expect. *Table 4—Before You Tell Your Story: Some Questions You May Want To Ask* presents some questions to help you gather the information you may need to make a decision about whether or not you want to tell your story.

Table 4

BEFORE YOU TELL YOUR STORY: SOME QUESTIONS YOU MAY WANT TO ASK

- When do you want me to speak? What day? What time? For how long?

- Where do you want me to speak? What site or city?

- Who is the audience? How many people will be there?

- Can you assure my confidentiality?

- What's the theme or topic?

- What part of my story do you want to hear?

- Is there a message you want me to leave them with?

- Is there reimbursement for child care and transportation?

- Is there an honorarium?

- Do you need an answer today? If not, by when?

If you decide to accept the invitation to speak, think carefully about the message you want your audience to remember. Your story is a rich and complex one. Be sure to pick the parts that are relevant to the situation or audience, and try to focus on two or three main points. Finally, organize your thoughts. You might even want to jot down an outline of your remarks. The most important thing, however, is to speak from your heart—be authentic, be respectful, and be constructive. You'll be wonderful!

For more guidance and ideas about speaking in public see the section on *Providing Training* on page 54.

Table 5

WHEN YOU TELL YOUR STORY: THINGS TO REMEMBER

- ✓ Know who your audience is and prepare with it in mind.
- ✓ Practice ahead of time.
- ✓ Use only two or three main points in your story.
- ✓ Use your own style.
- ✓ Use people-first language.
- ✓ Look at your audience.
- ✓ If you are comfortable doing so, share pictures of your child or family.
- ✓ Leave time for questions and answers.
- ✓ If you don't know the answer to a question, say so.
- ✓ Let the audience know your boundaries.
- ✓ Be honest.
- ✓ It may be helpful to put highlights of your story on note cards as a reference during the presentation—but avoid reading from them.
- ✓ Expect that some people who hear your story may be deeply moved. And remember, you might also feel emotional when you tell your story.
- ✓ Consider taking a friend, family member, or supporter with you. They can help with any problems that arise and sit up front so you can focus on a friendly face.

Plan for Challenges

As families move into advisory roles, they can expect to face certain challenges. Some of them have to do with working in new ways—remember, neither providers nor consumers have received adequate training in collaboration. Learning to communicate openly and honestly, and to handle the conflicts that will inevitably arise are all part of becoming an effective advisor. There are also logistical and practical challenges associated with consumer advisory roles. These require creativity and flexibility to overcome. Finally, some challenges may result from the stress associated with the advisory role. Taking care of yourself and seeking out the support you need are critical to success.

Managing Conflict

When you become an advisor, you will be working side-by-side with providers and other consumers to improve an overall program, institution, or system. In the interest of meeting that goal you will probably encounter opinions with which you disagree. Sometimes communication can break down and conflicts may emerge. That is natural and to be expected, but coping with conflicts can be hard work. Working through them constructively helps strengthen relationships and enables you to accomplish your goals. Learning the skills of effective conflict management is essential to your success as an advisor.

Words of Advice...
from Conni Wells

As an advisor, it's important to learn how to advocate tactfully and not in an adversarial way. Your role has changed. It's now become "how well can you convince someone that what they don't believe in is good for them." You have to learn how to get across new ideas.

Words of Advice...
from Sarah O'Brien

When you are struggling with conflict, don't take it to the top person, work the problem from where it started.

The first step in conflict management is personal self-awareness. Assess your strengths and areas of weakness in negotiating conflict and differences. Ask yourself the following questions:

- What do I bring to the table when differences exist?

- What did I learn growing up that might help or hinder my ability to value differences?

- How do my culture, background, and past experiences with the service system affect my ability to work with others?

- What patterns of behavior do I use when differences emerge?

The next step is to separate the person from the problem. Remember that consumers and providers are people first, and each brings a commitment to improving the system for children and families. Don't play the "blame game." It is not a matter of who is right and who is wrong. Agree that there is a disagreement, but recognize that finding a solution that works for everyone is the desired outcome. In many situations people bring very different perspectives. Trust that each person is struggling to understand and appreciate the others' viewpoints. Be sure to give the other person the benefit of the doubt.

Third, establish goals and priorities for solving the conflict. Everyone involved should define how she sees the problem and identify her priorities, without jumping too quickly to solutions or hard-and-fast positions. Based on the goals of each person, brainstorm as many options for solving the problem as possible. Try to be flexible and open to compromise.

Finally, strive to create options so that everyone "wins." Build in time for people to digest information and talk about their options with family or friends. Look for things you can agree on, and remember that time spent working through conflicts is time well spent. As you learn to constructively manage conflicts you strengthen your partnerships with your new colleagues and earn their respect.

Words of Advice...
from Conni Wells

If you're in a meeting or one-on-one with providers and find you disagree strongly, don't react at that moment. Focus on listening to be sure that you are clear about what you're hearing and not wrapped up in trying to come up with an answer right away. Ask questions to better understand the other person's viewpoint. After the meeting you have the opportunity to think through a response, brainstorm with someone else, and respond in writing.

Table 6

A CHECKLIST FOR MANAGING CONFLICT

- ❏ Handle differences in a timely manner, as soon after the event as possible.

- ❏ Stay in the present—do not focus on the past.

- ❏ Separate the event from the person, focusing on the incident at hand, not on personalities.

- ❏ Take responsibility for helping create the problem. Few conflicts are the sole responsibility of one person.

- ❏ Use "I" language, not "you", "we", or "they." Speak from your own experiences and take responsibility for your own ideas and feelings.

- ❏ Take care in making inferences and drawing conclusions. Describe the event as you experienced it, relate your feelings, and state the specific changes you would like to see.

- ❏ Listen carefully. Climb into the other person's shoes and try to understand his or her perspective, no matter how foreign it may be to your own thinking. Remember—others feel as passionately about their ideas and feelings as you do!

- ❏ Recognize others for their efforts and willingness to engage and care about each other.

Adapted from May, James (1995). Change: A Catalyst for Conflict and Growth. *Advances*, Vol. 2, No. 1, pp 18-19.

Overcoming Logistical and Bureaucratic Challenges

As families and other consumers participate more fully in advisory activities, they may encounter systems and organizational obstacles to their involvement. For example, many programs are unprepared to pay for consumers' expenses "up front." More typically, families are expected to wait for reimbursement for out-of-pocket expenses, a financial burden that many families cannot assume. Similarly, as programs begin to hire consumers in staff positions, they may not have flexible policies in place that take into account a family member's need to juggle the demands of her own or her child's illness. Fortunately, as more and more programs develop experience in working collaboratively with consumers at the policy and program level, solutions to these logistical challenges are emerging. Flexibility, the willingness to "learn as you go," and commitment to the process are essential to working through these inevitable challenges.

My thoughts:

Words of Advice...
from Katie Bond

One of the most important components of my settling into my job was the support of my supervisors. With them I had the opportunity to mold the position in ways I felt it should go.

Taking Care of Yourself

When families assume an advisory role they jump in with both feet. However, their enthusiasm and commitment—the very qualities that make them such wonderful advocates—can also lead to exhaustion and burn out. When only a few family members are serving in leadership roles, the likelihood of burn out increases. Family advisors must learn to monitor their own level of stress and fatigue and to take care of themselves. *Table 7—Strategies for Maintaining Your Balance* lists some strategies consumers can use to keep their advisory commitments manageable and meaningful.

While consumers must be vigilant about monitoring their own stress level, and building in some "down time" in their busy schedules, programs must also play a role in ensuring that consumers get the support they need to be successful in their new advisory roles. Flexible work hours, family-friendly personnel policies, and training for providers on the importance of collaborating with consumers can help consumers adjust to these new roles. Opportunities to meet with other family leaders for information sharing, problem-solving, and peer support should also be developed and supported.

Words of Advice...
from
Linda Horton-St. Hubert

Some days the women in our peer support program would wake up and say, "Today I can't focus on somebody else, or hearing about anyone else's issues. I need the day off." We developed a "quality of life" day. Every three months these peer supporters can take a day off to take care of themselves without prior arrangement with their supervisor.

Words of Advice...
from Mona Freedman

Getting support from other parents in leadership positions is really important. Every few months I schedule a meeting for the Parent Support Network Coordinators to get together to talk and share their successes and challenges.

Table 7
STRATEGIES FOR MAINTAINING YOUR BALANCE

- Evaluate your goals and priorities frequently. Are you meeting them? Is the time you're investing making a difference?

- Put your family first. Apply the twenty-year rule—will this have mattered to my family twenty years from now?

- Set priorities—decide what issues need to be tackled first.

- If you are in a paid staff position, strive for a clear, meaningful, and realistic job description that is flexible and can change over time.

- Set limits on travel, committee assignments, and conference presentations.

- Recognize that your colleagues—other parents and providers—have much they can teach you.

- Insist on having access to key leaders and decision makers.

- Find an experienced family member or provider to be your mentor.

- Stay in touch with other families. Involve other parents to ease the burden of representing the consumer perspective.

- Have patience, courage, and a sense of humor.

Serving as an Advisor: Six Roles You Can Play

Throughout *Words of Advice* we have presented information and exercises you can use to decide whether or not you want to serve as a policy and program advisor. The questions and issues addressed are applicable to the broad range of roles in which families may involve themselves. The remainder of this guide focuses on six common advisory roles. They are:

- Serving on an advisory board or committee

- Participating in a conference

- Providing training

- Testifying to legislators

- Offering peer support or mentoring

- Working in a paid staff or consultant position

Each section includes tips, tools, and the information you need to be successful in these activities.

If You're Serving On An Advisory Board Or Committee...

Many organizations and agencies have developed consumer advisory committees to provide input on policy and program issues. These committees can be made up solely of consumers or may have both consumers and providers as members. Some committees can be on-going, meeting regularly to offer guidance and feedback; others may have a very specific purpose and meet for only a short period of time.

Whatever the purpose of the advisory committee, you will need certain kinds of information and support to be able to serve effectively. Before you agree to participate, you should ask the following questions.

- What is the purpose of the advisory committee?
- How much time will it take? How frequent are the meetings? Will this be an ongoing committee or will it be short term?
- Will it involve travel?
- How many consumers will be on the committee? Who else is on the committee? What are their roles? What is the ratio of consumers to providers?
- What is my role?
- Will I get information and support so that I can participate effectively?

Words of Advice...
from the staff of Pilot Parent Partnerships

We've had a lot of experience serving on committees and boards. Here are some of the pointers we've come up with:

- *Seek out a buddy on the board and don't go to meetings alone, especially the first few times.*
- *Ask for a list of commonly used acronyms and terminology. Don't hesitate to ask what something means.*
- *Find out who is in charge in case concerns arise.*
- *Think through the best way to handle the sharing of family or personal information so you can make your points most effectively.*
- *Know the subtle rules that make a difference—where to sit, what is done about lunch and breaks, the best time to arrive and leave.*
- *It's okay not to know. Becoming an active participant takes time. Listen. Take notes.*
- *Ask lots of questions.*

- Is reimbursement available for my time and expenses—travel, per diem, postage, phone calls, child care? Is it available ahead of time? If not, how long will I have to wait?

- Is there a formal orientation for new members? If so how does it happen?

- What has the committee accomplished?

> ***Words of Advice...***
> *from Glen Turner*
>
> *As a Dad, be aware that at some meetings you may be the only man.*

If, after gathering this preliminary information, you decide to join the advisory committee, the ideas in *Table 8—Tips For Serving On An Advisory Committee* on the next page will help you get the most out of your participation.

Table 8
TIPS FOR SERVING ON AN ADVISORY COMMITTEE

- Ask for directions to the meeting. Allow plenty of time to get there.

- Find out if parking is available and where to park.

- Get a phone number to leave with your family or sitter.

- Read materials you've received ahead of time.

- Ask the members to introduce themselves if they haven't.

- Take notes—they will help you remember later.

- Ask questions—there is no such thing as a dumb question. Someone else probably has the same question and feels too shy to ask.

- Ask for explanations of acronyms or confusing terminology.

- Observe body language—you'll pick up a lot of clues about how people are feeling.

- Attending regularly will help you to clarify the issues, understand the group's dynamics, and learn who is an ally.

- Know yourself—be clear about your values and priorities.

- Get to know the providers and learn about their perspectives.

- Offer to share your community resources and networks.

- Listen.

In addition to general advisory boards, you may be asked to serve on a committee with a very specific function. These might include steering committees, ethics committees, research committees, and personnel committees.

Steering Committees. Steering committees provide oversight, determine rules, and set the direction for a particular initiative, program, or institution. The members of steering committees are often the chairpersons of a number of different subcommittees. Steering committees tend to operate rather formally.

Ethics Committees. Ethics committees are responsible for determining standards of right and wrong. In health care settings, these committees provide consultation and, sometimes, mediation, on complex medical treatment and research issues. Often ethics committees are asked to consult on end-of-life decisions, or when there are disagreements between patients and their families and medical personnel. Consumers bring valuable perspectives and experiences to the deliberations of ethics committees.

Research Committees. The primary function of a research committee is to protect children, families, and other research subjects from harm. Committees do this by ensuring that a proposed research

---

Words of Advice...
from
Linda Horton-St. Hubert
and Rosemary Johnson

We found ourselves being invited to many different meetings, so we devised a plan that would let us share these advisory roles and not be stretched too thin. We go to meetings together, and keep each other up-to-date if one of us misses a meeting. We only have one vote between us, but the plan we've worked out means there's always a consumer at the table when important decisions are made.

project does not cause any physical or emotional discomfort, and by ensuring that informed consent is a part of all research activities. Increasingly, research committees are also taking a proactive role in designing research that protects the rights of participants and makes a worthwhile contribution to science. Consumer participation on research committees can help to ensure that research designs and research questions are practical, appropriate, and respectful of families.

Personnel Committees. Consumers also may be asked to serve on personnel or staff recruitment committees. These committees are charged with recruiting, interviewing, and selecting new staff members. Consumers perspectives are invaluable in hiring and training staff who can work in effective partnerships with families.

My thoughts:

_____

_____

_____

_____

_____

_____

If You're Attending A Conference…

Participating in a conference in a city away from home can be an exciting experience providing you with both opportunity and responsibility. You may have the opportunity to increase your knowledge of your own or your child's health condition. You may have a chance to meet other families whose children have similar needs and share similar interests. You also may have the opportunity to learn about how care for children and their families is being delivered in other parts of the country.

You have the responsibility to follow the guidelines and policies of the agency that is funding your travel. Typically, they have specific guidelines for allowable travel expenses, necessary receipts, and timelines for reimbursement. Ask about these guidelines before you leave.

If you receive additional financial support from another organization, make sure you are clear on what expenses that organization will cover. Of course, it is not ethical to "double dip" (such as having your hotel bill paid twice by two different organizations).

Most agencies never reimburse for:

- materials not included in conference registrations costs, such as audiotapes of sessions.

- meals not included or agreed on ahead of time

- "over budget" meals (you are likely to have a set amount to use for meals)

- alcoholic beverages

- entertainment expenses (such as in-room movies, trips to nightclubs)

- personal telephone expenses

- souvenirs

The following guidelines for attending a conference were first developed by Michigan's Parent Participation Program and adapted for *Words of Advice*.

Travel Tips

Here are a few travel tips to make your trip smoother.

- Label all your luggage inside and out.

- Don't check luggage containing medication, prescription eye glasses, or other items you can't live without. Keep important items in your carry-on bag.

- Customary tipping for hotel shuttle assistance, bag handling, or curbside service is $1 per bag.

- If you need a special meal on a flight offering food service, order from the airline at least two days in advance. You can call the airline reservation line to do this.

- Be sure to take a picture ID with you for airport check-in.

- Be at the airport at least one hour before your flight's departure. If your flight is canceled, try to re-book at the gate.

- If you miss your flight, it's usually possible to re-book on the next flight. However, you may have to pay some extra costs. Ask about going "stand-by" on a later flight.

- Hotels typically ask for a credit card when checking in. Many require one for possible in-room charges, such as telephone service or movies. If you don't have a credit card you can usually ask the hotel to block those services or you may pay a deposit in cash. A $20 deposit is typical.

- You can use the hotel's pay phone to avoid in-room phone charges. Many hotels add a $.75 to $1.50 fee to each phone call you make from your room — even local calls! A prepaid calling card that can be purchased ahead of time may make calling home easier for you.

- Please note that snacks in the mini-bar refrigerator that may be in your room are **very expensive!**

Transportation to and from the Airport

You will need cash to cover your expenses to and from the airport. You can usually find a shuttle service to take you to the hotel from the airport. Taxi cabs are often very expensive, but you may be able to share the cost with other people attending the meeting. When you arrive at the hotel, ask about transportation back to the airport. Often hotels in large cities have shuttle service for a fee or even for free.

Coordination at Home

Be sure you have arranged for emergencies at home. When you get to the hotel, call home and leave the hotel phone number and your room number. You can also get the conference phone number from the conference staff so that you can be reached in an emergency.

What to Bring

You may be wondering what to bring. Each conference is different. At some conferences, everyone wears business clothes. At others, people wear casual, comfortable clothes. You may want to ask someone who has gone to the conference before what people typically wear. You may also want to bring fun, comfortable clothes to wear in the evening, for walking around town, or just hanging out. Most hotels have swimming pools and/or exercise equipment for hotel guests, so be sure to tuck a swim suit and workout clothes into your bag.

While You are at the Conference.

After you check in to the hotel, find out where the conference is being held. There will probably be signs telling you where to go. Check in with the conference organizers. You will receive conference materials that tell you when events start and where they will be held. If you read these ahead of time, you will be able to choose what sessions you want to attend and which speakers you would like to hear. If you are attending with another consumer advisor, be sure to divide up so you can go to different sessions and double the amount of information to take back home.

You may want to take notes during the conference to help you remember what you heard. If there are handouts, be sure to take some home. Some conferences also sell audiotapes of the sessions. If your budget allows, you may want to purchase several.

When you return home, be sure to meet with other families and providers to share what you have learned.

Words of Advice...
from Molly Cole

Don't maintain ownership of information: Share and network. Be a team player and collaborate.

If You're Providing Training…

Telling your story on a panel of speakers at a meeting or conference is one of the ways that you may be sharing your expertise. A panel is a group of people speaking together on the same topic from different perspectives. You may be the only parent on the panel or you may be one of several.

Preparing for a Panel Presentation

Listed below are some tips for preparing a panel presentation.

- Find out how much time you have.

- Ask about the specific topics to be discussed by each panel member.

- Ask who else will be on the panel and what perspectives they will present. Find out the order people will be speaking in—who will be first, second, last? If possible, talk to the other panelists.

- Talk with someone you trust to help you brainstorm ideas for your presentation.

Words of Advice…
from
Linda Horton-St. Hubert

I tell my story to educate, to inspire, to enhance understanding, and to heal myself.

- Develop your talk around one or two key issues that your story will illustrate. You may want to organize your talk around the following ideas:

    - Describe your child and family and one or two experiences you have had being a family member of a child with special needs.

    - Talk about what you want or need from providers. Talk about what went well and what specifically helped. Describe the kinds of services or approaches that were most supportive. Describe what didn't go well and what you wish would have happened. Be specific.

- Write down your key points so you can refer to them easily.

- If you are using handouts, check to see how many you will need.

- Practice your presentation to see how long it is and to get more comfortable saying it aloud.

- Bring a picture of your child and family to pass around, if you would like. Or, you can have your family photograph copied on an overhead transparency. It costs about $5, but looks very professional.

Organizing a Formal Presentation

As an advisor, one of your responsibilities may be to speak to audiences of families and providers at meetings or conferences. Here are some key points to keep in mind when you are developing a presentation.

Plan the logistics. Plan the logistics ahead of time. Find out where you need to be and at what time. Ask about parking or other transportation.

Let them know what audiovisual equipment you might need. Will you need a microphone, overhead projector, or flip chart? Will you be seated at a table or standing in front of the room? How will the participants be seated?

Be sure to discuss ahead of time any stipend or honorarium and travel expenses.

Send written confirmation of your understanding of the request, time, place, date, the audiovisual equipment to be provided, and reimbursement.

Give yourself plenty of time to get there. Call for directions if you are unfamiliar with the area. Don't be surprised if you need to rearrange chairs, tables, or audiovisual equipment to make you and/or the audience more comfortable. Be sure you have everything you will need: masking tape, flip charts, magic markers.

Plan your presentation. Organize your ideas. Think about what you want to say. Some people find it helps to write their whole presentation down; others find it more helpful just to write a few notes to refer to while they are speaking.

Be yourself. When you are preparing your presentation, use your strengths to prepare your talk.

Identify your goals. What two or three main points do you want the audience to remember after your talk? Develop your presentation around those key points.

Remember that stories have a beginning or introduction, a middle, and an end. In the introduction, you can introduce yourself and tell why you are here. At the end, you may want to summarize your story by highlighting the key points you made.

Use your sense of humor. If you have a funny story about your family or child, use it to highlight a point or to introduce or summarize your presentation.

Know your audience. Try to find out as much as you can about your audience, including their backgrounds or disciplines, their past training, and what they've heard before on the topic. Be flexible enough so you can emphasize points that particularly interest your audience.

Involve the audience in your presentation. When questions are raised, turn them over to the entire group before answering yourself.

Use handouts. Frequently, participants like to take notes. It is really hard to talk to the tops of people's heads. Having handouts helps keep people focused on your presentation rather than trying to write furiously to keep up with what you're saying. Simple handouts can include a description of your family and some family pictures. Many copy centers can make handouts for a small cost.

Practice your presentation. If you will be using overheads or slides, practice using them. Practice participatory exercises not familiar to you. Anticipate some of the questions you may be asked. Think about how you would respond.

For additional tips about speaking in public see the section on *Telling Your Story* on page 31.

My thoughts:

_____

_____

_____

_____

_____

If You're Testifying To Legislators...

Some families share their stories with elected officials or bureaucrats to influence the outcome of bills and laws being passed or funded. The following tips were adapted from those developed by Terry Ohlson-Martin & Robert Madisen for Family Voices.

Be yourself. Someone asked you to testify because of who you are and what you and your family have experienced with the service system. Start with your name, where you come from, and where you work. Be clear about what organization you represent if you are there on behalf of a group.

Tell your story. The real, personal examples of your family's experiences are what set you apart from others who may provide testimony.

- Talk about the daily challenges you and your family face because of your condition or your child's.

- Use pictures or graphics. Passing around a picture of your family makes your points even more real.

- Provide written testimony. If possible, type it and have enough copies for the entire committee. Include your name, address, and phone number. Don't expect anyone to read more than a page during the hearing. If you need or want to submit long reports, give them to the staff of the people hearing testimony—preferably, a few days before the hearing.

- Provide your ideas on possible solutions. What makes a difference for you and your family? Try to be practical and specific.

Words of Advice...
from Glen Turner

When I provide testimony or speak at a meeting, instead of business cards I pass out my family's photograph with my name, address, and phone number printed on the back. They don't forget us!

Be factual. Always tell the truth or risk losing credibility.

Be polite, courteous, and respectful.

Control your temper. If you are concerned that you may lose control, provide written testimony only.

Be concrete. If there is specific legislation involved, explain how it will affect your child and family.

Try not to be afraid. You are talking to people who may have experienced similar situations within their own families or through friends.

Keep it short. One page written or five minutes spoken is enough.

Be prepared for questions. It's okay to say "I don't know."

Try not to be redundant. If someone has said something before you, agree with that person, but don't repeat.

Before you go:

- ✓ Practice, practice, practice.

- ✓ Allow plenty of time to be at the hearing—a half day at least. It helps to get a sense of what's being said before and after you testify.

- ✓ Be prepared for delays and changes in the schedule or the amount of time allotted to you. Prepare remarks that you can amend if you need to.

- ✓ Wear nice clothes that make you feel good.

After the hearing:

- ✓ Thank members of the committee, especially anyone who was especially helpful or sympathetic to your issues.

- ✓ Establish relationships with appropriate policy makers and their support staff.

- ✓ Encourage and support others to testify—don't always be the only one there.

If You're Supporting Other Families…

One of the most important roles families can play is providing support to other families. Indeed, becoming a peer supporter is often the first opportunity that consumers have to make the system of care better.

You already have the most important qualifications for helping other families: your experiences with your own children and family. When you share your experiences in a matter-of-fact way and share your pride in your children and family, you show by your example that it is possible to survive difficult experiences and live a happy and productive life. This is a powerful message. It is the way you bring strength and hope to other families.

Another way you can help families is by providing an opportunity for them to talk about their experiences and by really *listening* to them. People who have faced challenges or struggled with difficult emotions say that the most helpful thing anyone can do for them is to listen—not try to provide solutions to their problems. By using active listening and other communication techniques, methods that have been used by mental health professionals for many years, you can become a very effective support person for other families.

Active Listening

Active listening means trying to understand exactly what another person is saying and letting that person know you have understood. When you are actively listening, you pay attention both to what is being said and to the feelings expressed. The basic elements of active listening are presented in *Table 9—Techniques for Being an Active Listener.*

Table 9
TECHNIQUES FOR BEING AN ACTIVE LISTENER

Be attentive. Pay close attention to what is being said. Listen with your whole self by using eye contact, a nod of the head, or a hand gesture that encourages the speaker to go on. Even the way you sit or stand lets the other person know you are interested.

Be impartial. This is the most difficult part of active listening. It means not agreeing, disagreeing, or even sharing any opinion you may have. It's hard to keep our emotions and feelings in check and remain totally open about what the other person is saying. Remember the purpose of active listening is to understand the *other* person. Be open to other people's values and perspectives.

Reflect back. Use the same or similar words to repeat the speaker's idea back to him or her. For example—Speaker: "I'm really mad about my clinic visit today." Listener: "It sounds like you didn't like what happened today." This technique helps the speaker know that you are interested and that you would like more information.

Listen for feelings. Often the feelings that the speaker shares are the most important part of their message. Listen carefully for those feelings and acknowledge them. You can say…"You seem angry" or "You seem to have some concerns about how your clinic visit went today" or "You sound frustrated."

Summarize. Pick out what you think were the most important parts of the speaker's message. Repeat them back to the speaker to be sure that you understand and to let the speaker know that you understood.

Adapted from Edelman, L. E., Greenland, B. M., & Mills, B. L. (1992). *Family-centered communication skills: Facilitator's guide.* St. Paul, MN: Pathfinder Resources.

Sharing Personal Experiences

Family-to-family support means families use their own experiences as a guide to help other families in similar situations. The following guidelines are useful for determining when to use your own experiences with other families. Sharing personal experiences can be useful:

- To introduce yourself to another family.
- To let others know they are not alone.
- To help other families discuss a problem they may find difficult to talk about.
- To show acceptance of a family member's feelings and to build rapport.
- To reinforce another family's decisions or actions.
- To introduce a new topic.
- To illustrate a point.

It is very important to stress that everyone is different and will find unique answers to their own problems. When using your own experience as an example, you might say, "This worked for me, but I can't say that it will work for you. I just want to share it with you because it might be something you have not thought of yet."

Words of Advice...
from Bruce Orr

Often times fathers do not get a chance to or take time to grieve. This may appear as anger or depression. Dads are trying to be strong so moms can lose it. Big boys don't cry and sometimes men need permission to cry. One way to support dads is to give them some time and space to grieve the loss of the dreams they had for their children.

In sharing personal experiences, it is important to remember that no one can know exactly how another person is feeling. Instead of saying "I know how you feel," say, "I have had similar feelings (or experiences) myself."

Table 10

SOME HELPFUL THINGS TO SAY

- It's OK to feel sad. You have a right to feel that way.
- You are not alone. I will be here for you.
- I don't think you are crazy. But dealing with all these things can sure seem crazy.
- What can I do to help you sort out the situation?
- There are some resource programs that might be able to help you.
- I don't have all the answers, but maybe I can make a few suggestions.
- Take one thing at a time.
- You will do it better than you think.
- Always remember it is your right and your responsibility to get all the information you need and want.
- Above all, remember you know yourself and your child best.
- Love and enjoy yourself, your child, and your family.

Giving Advice

Families in supporting roles are often asked for their advice. However, giving advice can sometimes do more harm than good. Although you may feel that you have a lot of advice to give, there are dangers associated with giving advice. For instance:

- You may be offering a solution before you know the real issue.

- You may not have all the information to understand the problem.

- The person may need more time to work through and share her feelings before working on a solution.

- Giving advice may prevent the person from developing her own answers.

- Getting advice makes some people feel patronized.

Suggesting options rather than giving advice is a very important skill in family-to-family support. One of your goals is to empower other families to make their own choices. Some of the things you can do instead of giving advice are presented in *Table 11—What To Do Instead of Giving Advice*.

Table 11

WHAT TO DO INSTEAD OF GIVING ADVICE

- **Find out more information.**
  "I know you are really upset about this, but maybe you could tell me more about what you're thinking."

- **Offer your own or others' experiences.**
  Share an experience when you were able to work through a similar problem.

- **Refer the person to a professional.**
  Remind them that there are many skilled professionals who can help them work through this particular situation.

- **Help them think through the problem and approaches to solving it.**

- **End the conversation at an appropriate break point.**
  Suggest stopping for a time to think about what has been discussed. Be sure to agree when you will talk again, even as soon as the next day.

- **Simply say, "I don't know".**
  Rather than give advice that can be harmful, simply say that you don't know.

- **Be quiet!**
  Remember just listening will help the other person feel supported and better able to find solutions to her own problems.

Adapted from *Support parent training: Facilitator's guide* (1994). Michigan Parent Participation Program.

If You're Considering A Paid Staff or Consultant Position…

Over the last two decades a number of programs have hired consumers in paid staff positions. While this trend is growing, it is still the exception, rather than the rule. Therefore, if you want to find a paid consumer position, you will probably need to take the initiative to create one. You may need to :

- Identify the needs of the agency, clinic, or hospital that could be met by hiring a family member.

- Write a brief proposal for a specific program or position based on the organizational needs you've identified.

- Write your own job description and present it to the organization with a good supportive argument for why they should hire you.

- Anticipate and be prepared to respond to objections that you may encounter.

- Find a friend to support your proposal—preferably someone from within the system.

- When you present your ideas take along another family member who has been, or is in, a similar position.

Words of Advice…
from Sarah O'Brien

I think there are certain positive attitudes and behaviors that go along with being in a paid parent position. You need to be energetic and enthusiastic about your role—and to be up-front and honest with everyone. You must believe in the services your agency provides and have some loyalty to the agency…but always remember that you are also a representative for families.

- Have documentation of the benefits of a consumer consultant position.

- Offer information about other successful parent consultants to support your position.

- Show what other consumers are doing and the pay scale for those jobs.

- Explore funding sources and develop a proposal for funding your position.

- Be willing to approach several agencies, programs, or hospitals.

Because these paid consumer positions are a fairly new phenomenon, we're still learning what it takes to make them successful. Among the components that consumers have identified as needing to be in place are:

- commitment from the top;

- policies that allow for creative and flexible involvement in paid positions —working from home, job sharing, access to computers, FAX, teleconferencing;

Words of Advice...
from
Felecia Jordan Da-Silva

We hired two parents to share the coordinator's position at Project Uptown, part of the Family Support Network of Michigan. Job sharing has allowed these parents to bring their very different skills and experiences to the job and to balance family responsibilities.

Words of Advice...
from Katie Bond

From the start, they made it clear that they understood I needed time for doctor's appointments, etc. They were willing to be flexible about my working from home or taking leaves of absence.

- clear role definition and job descriptions developed over time with a supervisor;
- adequate pay and reimbursement mechanisms;
- frequent contact with other families;
- support and leadership from a mentor;
- support from staff;
- ongoing supportive supervision with clear expectations; and
- the ability to take a leave of absence if illness occurs.

My thoughts:

_____
_____
_____
_____
_____
_____

Developing Your Resumé

As you become more involved in consumer advisory roles, you may be asked for your resumé. Many family members have not thought about how to translate the skills they have gained as consumers into a resumé. On the next page is a sample resumé that shows how a parent's experiences with her child and in the community can be organized to reflect the vast amount of skill and expertise acquired in caring for a child with special health care needs.

Table 12

SAMPLE RESUMÉ

Ima Consumer
1234 West Main Street • Apt. #24 • Anytown, NY 13456 • 111-555-1234

EXPERIENCE

1989 - Present   **Case manager, developmental therapist, and advocate for my child with multiple health care needs.**
- Implement multi-disciplinary, home-based care program for my child with special health care needs and family.
- Collaborate with providers in developing care plan for my child and family.
- Coordinate care plan among 6 medical specialists and 3 therapists.
- Negotiate with education system to obtain needed services for my child.
- Administer and regulate medicines.
- Maintain medical records and complete documentation.
- Negotiate financial arrangements with health care and medical providers.
- Recruit, hire, and train respite care workers.

1992- Present   **Coordinator, "Families United" Family Support Network**
- Coordinate activities of 25 member community-based family support network.
- Provide peer support to over 100 families who have children with special needs.
- Advocate for access to services in community.
- Present information on children with special needs and their families to local, regional, and national audiences.
- Attend state and national conferences with families and professionals.

1994-Present   **Member, "Holy Hospital" Family Advisory Board**
- Participate in monthly advisory board meetings to set and review hospital policies related to children and their families.
- Present information to hospital personnel on children with special needs and their families.

EDUCATION

1975 - 1977   Anytown Community College, Business Management, AA Degree
1985   Northeast Parent Leadership Institute, Parent-to-Parent Support Training

RELATED EXPERIENCES

1990-Present   Volunteer, Holy Hospital Family Resource Library
1994 -1995   President, Anytown Elementary School PTA
1993   Coordinator, Girl Scout Cookie Sales Committee

Ready or Not? 15 Questions to Ask Yourself

Now that you've read *Words of Advice*, you may be excited about taking on an advisory role in your community. The statements on the next page will help you assess your readiness and identify areas where you may need additional knowledge and training. Read each statement and circle the number on the scale that best reflects your abilities and understanding. Your self-assessment will help you plan next steps in your process of becoming an advisor.

Activity 9
BECOMING AN ADVISOR: A SELF-ASSESSMENT INVENTORY

	You bet!		Not yet
1. I can name at least five benefits to having families in advisory roles.	1	2	3
2. I can list at least five advisory roles for consumers.	1	2	3
3. I can list five barriers to consumers serving in advisory roles.	1	2	3
4. I can name three strategies for increasing family involvement at the policy and program level.	1	2	3
5. If I want to, I know how and where to join a family-to-family support group.	1	2	3
6. I can list two places where consumers are already serving in advisory roles.	1	2	3
7. I know where to find information about opportunities for participating as an advisor.	1	2	3
8. I know at least one provider who could help me develop an advisory role.	1	2	3
9. I know a veteran parent who can be my mentor.	1	2	3
10. I have thought about telling my story and have identified the parts I feel comfortable sharing.	1	2	3
11. I have some ideas about where I can gain additional skills and information to make me a better advisor.	1	2	3
12. I have developed a resumé that shows how my experiences as a consumer have prepared me to be an advisor.	1	2	3
13. I know how to stay in touch with other families in the community.	1	2	3
14. I have identified the practical and emotional supports I will need to be an effective advisor.	1	2	3
15. I know the questions to ask before I agree to serve as an advisor.	1	2	3

In Conclusion

We hope after reading *Words of Advice* you have a better understanding of the benefits and challenges of serving as a policy and program advisor. And we hope that you feel inspired to find opportunities to use your experiences as a consumer to help improve the service system for other families.

Remember that being an effective advisor is a process that occurs over time—and it starts with you. Think through your commitment to this exciting work, determine the supports you'll need, build your skills, and learn to be a constructive collaborator both with providers and with other consumers. You have a unique contribution to make. Go for it!

My thoughts:

_____

_____

_____

_____

_____

Words of Advice...
from Linda Horton-St. Hubert and Geneva Morrison

10 STEPS FOR BEING A SUCCESSFUL ADVISOR

1. ***Begin with yourself.*** *You can't participate effectively as an advisor until you have yourself together. Think about how you present yourself. Develop an understanding of how you come across to others. Strive to be positive.*
2. ***Learn about the community.*** *Learn who the people and programs are and what they do.*
3. ***Develop the big picture.*** *Educate yourself about the issues that concern all people affected by the service system. Think beyond your own family.*
4. ***Develop new skills.*** *Attend conferences (especially the free ones). Learn about computers, about public speaking, about how organizations work.*
5. ***Assume the best about people.*** *Providers are not the enemy. Build bridges, don't burn them.*
6. ***Learn to collaborate****—with providers and other consumers.*
7. ***Be prepared.*** *Do your homework. Read what they send you. Ask questions.*
8. ***Learn to say "no."*** *Don't take on too much. Know when you need a break.*
9. ***Share the spotlight.*** *Suggest other families who can also participate in advisory activities. Provide encouragement to them.*
10. ***Go to the dump-yard.*** *Get rid of old prejudices and stereotypes. Keep an open mind and an open heart.*

Who Are The Advisors?

The advisors who worked with us to develop this publication offered much insight about what it means to work in these new roles. In addition to the advisory roles described below, they are all parents or grandparents of children with special needs, or are themselves consumers of health services.

Katie Bond, Parent Consultant at MassCare, coordinates family activities and facilitates the involvement of families in policy and program activities.

Molly Cole is the Director of the Family Center at Connecticut Children's Medical Center.

Bev Crider is the Director of the Parent Participation Program, Department of Community Health, Detroit Michigan and is on the board of directors of Family Voices.

Nancy DiVenere is Director of Parent to Parent of Vermont where she coordinates a project to teach medical students about the needs of families who have children with special needs.

Faye Eldar, Illinois Family Voices Coordinator, frequently advises state agencies and organizations on issues related to health care financing and families of children with special health care needs.

Mona Freedman is the Family Support Network Coordinator for the Maryland Infants and Toddler's Program.

Linda Horton-St. Hubert is the Women and Family Advocate at the Institute for Family-Centered Care.

Rosemary Johnson is the women's outreach worker at Johns Hopkins University Hospital.

Felecia Jordan Da-Silva is the coordinator of Project Uptown at Michigan's Family Support Network.

Geneva Morrison serves on the Ryan White Planning Council in Newark and frequently speaks to national audiences on issues related to HIV.

Sarah O'Brien works at South Carolina's Department of Health and Environmental Control, Division of Children's Rehabilitative Services as the Parent Liaison.

Bruce Orr is a parent member of Delaware's ICC and speaks both nationally and locally on issues related to children with special needs and African American fathers.

Parent Pilot Partnerships is a resource center for parents of children with special needs. They provide information, support, and technical assistance to parents in Arizona.

Virginia Ross is the first family member to serve as chair of the board for Circle of Care, a consortium of organizations that serve children, families, and adults with HIV in Philadelphia.

Glen Turner is a parent member of his state's ICC and the PTA president at his children's school.

Conni Wells serves as the Parent Consultant for Florida Children's Medical Services Program in Tallahassee. Conni speaks nationally on issues related to health care financing for children with special health care needs.

Resources

The following resources may be useful as you develop your skills as an advisor.

Publications

Essential Allies: Families as Advisors
by Elizabeth S. Jeppson & Josie Thomas

Families as Advisors: A Training Guide for Collaboration
by Elizabeth S. Jeppson & Josie Thomas

Making Connections: Building Family Support Networks for Families Living with HIV
by Josie Thomas, Linda Horton, Ibby Jeppson, & Jenny Jones

The Parent Leadership Program Training Manual
by Joan Blough, Patt Brown, Sharon Dietrich, and Bryn Fortune

> **Available from:**
> Institute for Family-Centered Care
> 7900 Wisconsin Avenue, Suite 405
> Bethesda, MD 20814
> 301-652-0281

Parents as Policy-Makers: A Handbook for Effective Collaboration
by Richard W. Hunter

> **Available from:**
> Research and Training Center on Family Support and Children's Mental Health
> Portland State University
> P.O. Box 751
> Portland, OR 97201-0751
> 503-725-4040

Telling Your Family Story…Parents as Presenters
(video and video guide)
by Stacy King

> **Available from:**
> Parent Projects
> Waisman Center, Room 231
> University of Wisconsin-Madison
> 1500 Highland Avenue
> Madison, WI 53705-2280
> 608-265-2063

Internet sites

Federation for Children with Special Needs

The web site has information for parents about special education and family support. Technical assistance for parent training and information centers is included. The ICC Parent Leadership Project featured on the web site provides leadership training and mentoring opportunities for parent leaders serving on ICCs.

http://www.fcsn.org

Research and Training Center on Family Support and Children's Mental Health

The web site features current activities of the center, excellent articles on a variety of topics related to children's mental health, and an on-line version of their innovative newsletter, *Focal Point*. Information about research related to family participation at the policy level is included.

http://www-adm.pdx.edu/user/rri/rtc/

The National Parent Network on Disabilities

Information and resources for parents to help them influence and affect policy issues concerning the needs of people with disabilities and their families. Excellent links to many other web sites.

http://www.npnd.org